Dear BIG BROTHER,

You are going to be a great older brother! The twins will be your new best friends. You will share lots of hugs, laughs, and great times with your baby siblings.

When the babies are born, things will change a little in your house. But one thing that will never change is how much you are LOVED!

Mommy and Daddy may be extra tired after the new babies come!

Twins are either IDENTICAL or FRATERNAL.

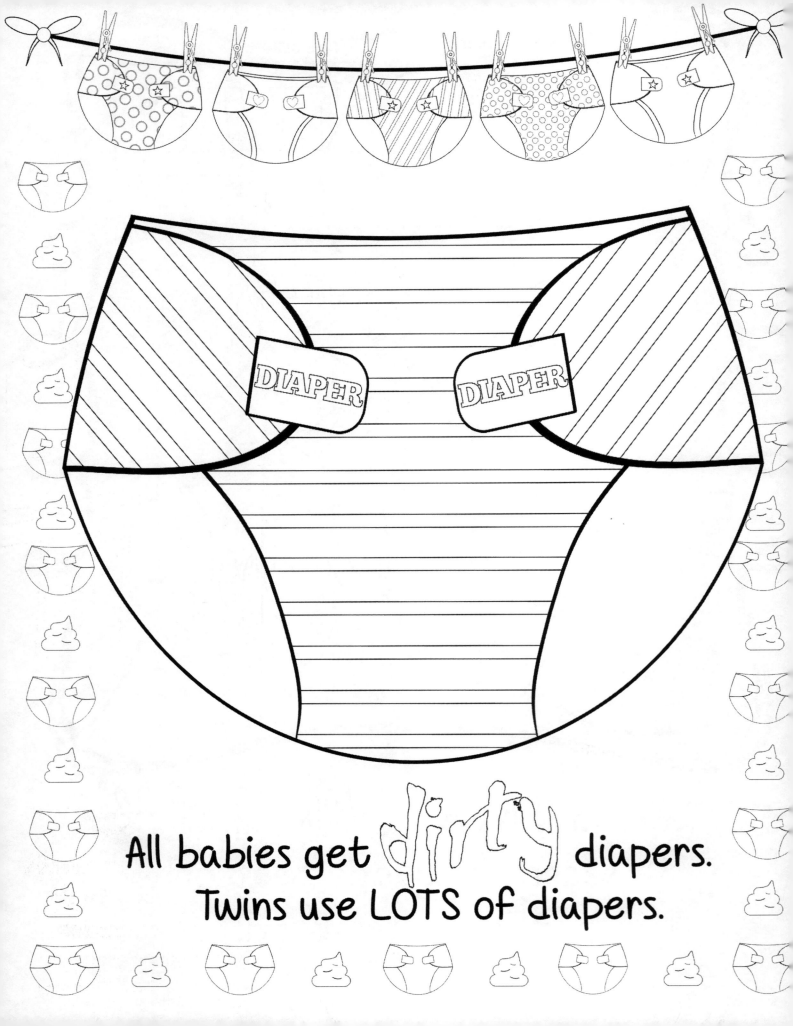

Sometimes these are STINKY diapers. The twins will get a fresh diaper on a changing table. They may cry and fuss.

Big Brother Tip: Sing your favorite song to the twins to cheer them up!

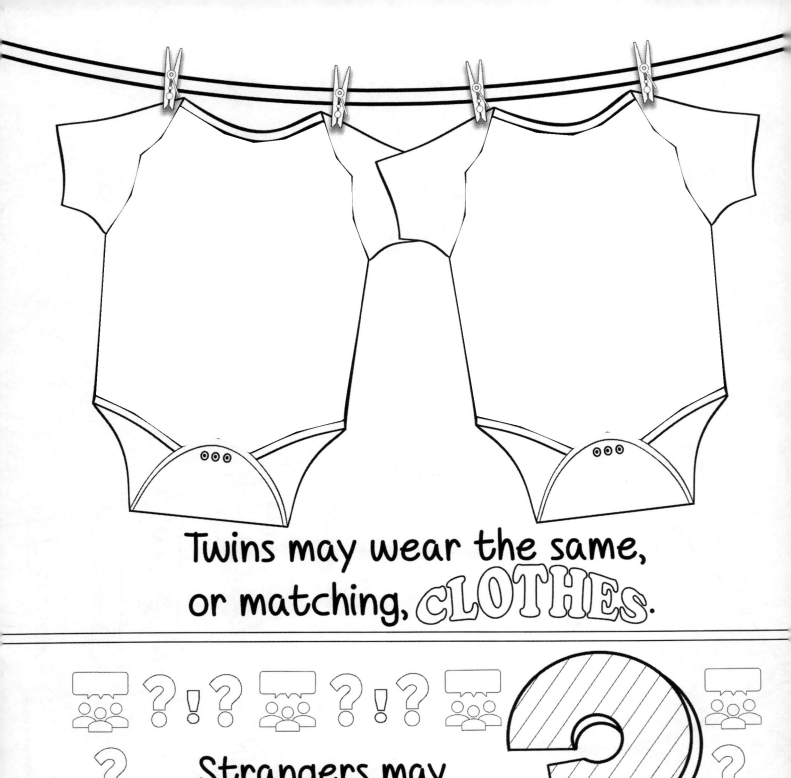

Twins may wear the same, or matching, CLOTHES.

Strangers may ask lots of QUESTIONS about the twins.

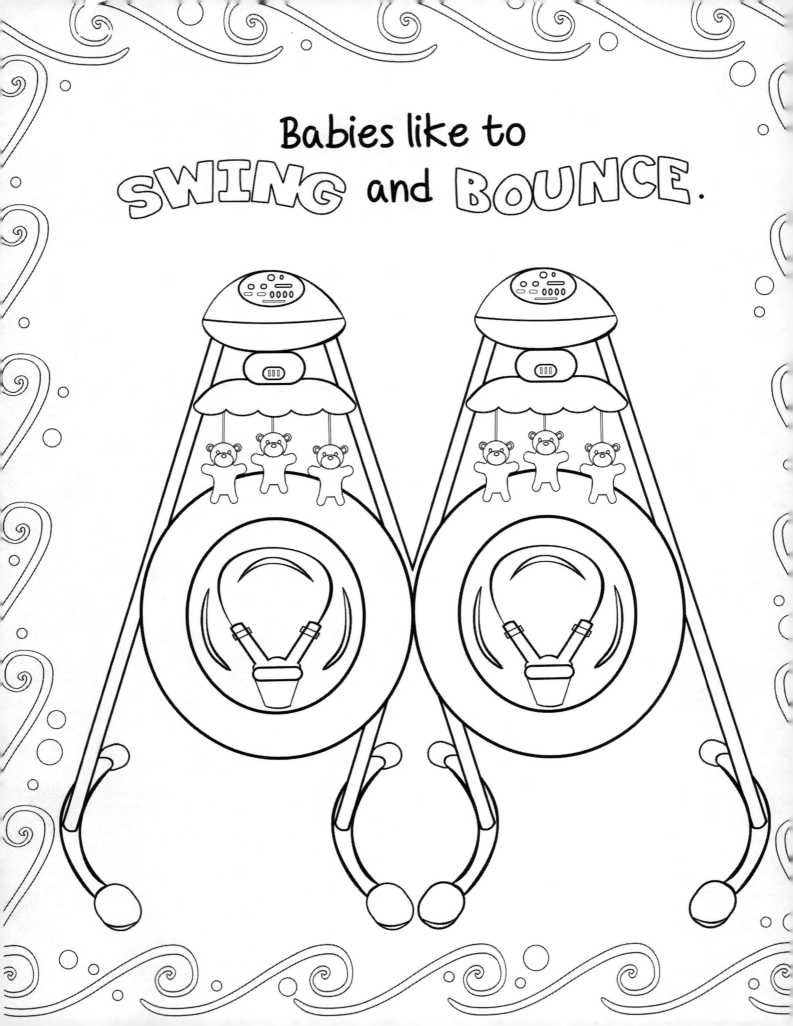

You can play games with the twins. Babies like to play PEEK-a-BOO.

and "How BIG are Twins?" game.

SO BIG!

There will be lots of special moments with your baby twins like: The first BATH,

Draw a picture of your twin siblings.

Match the objects to the baby.

 Can you help the twins find their way to the crib?

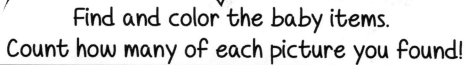

Find and color the baby items.
Count how many of each picture you found!

Complete the PATTERN.

Look at the pattern below. Use the box to complete the pattern.

Alphabet Challenge

Can you find baby items that start with each of these letters?

A _____
B _____
C _____
D _____
E _____
F _____
G _____
H _____
I _____
J _____
K _____
L _____
M _____

N _____
O _____
P _____
Q _____
R _____
S _____
T _____
U _____
V _____
W _____
X _____
Y _____
Z _____

TWINS WORD FIND

Find twin baby words. Circle/highlight the words in the puzzle.

```
N M Q B I D J Q S I E C M T F K R F X D
U I D E N T I C A L J M U S Q I U S Y D
N R N Q K C Q U U Q S F N T C A J V U S
S V U M P R W C L S H D H Z E I Z R R T
U K D J X S B U M J P U S V Q N H F A O
D B T C F Z T D G W B A E B N J E Z Q R
Y S H W G R V D T T J L C L C C Q S A Y
U W F P I D I L O H D I T Z H A O P S T
U A R R Z N G E S V O P M M I T M X X I
Y D D T A Y S S N T F Y A E L C I Y A M
D D V V T T D D C D R D T E D N R K I E
N L X N L J E M O S S O M S R L A D I I
M E L D V J P R W U A F L F E C C N G X
Z I W X Y B H A N Y B X O L N A L Q E T
Y R S B W S G L I A X L D R E Z E C B W
Z I J X O H B R W R L S E G E R Z A O T
R H B Y D R J I N F A N T S X V F W G V
A F E J M D N K K X M G I G G L E H O P
L U L L A B Y S J D S N R B C O L R K R
C T U B B Y H D M M N G N X E Z E X V G
```

Identical	Dual	Swaddle	Infants
Fraternal	BOGO	Cuteness	Lullaby
Twins	Newborns	Giggle	Children
Double	Miracle	Storytime	Cuddles
Pair	Friends Forever	Stroller	Tubby

SPOT THE DIFFERENCES
Can you find the 8 differences between the pictures?

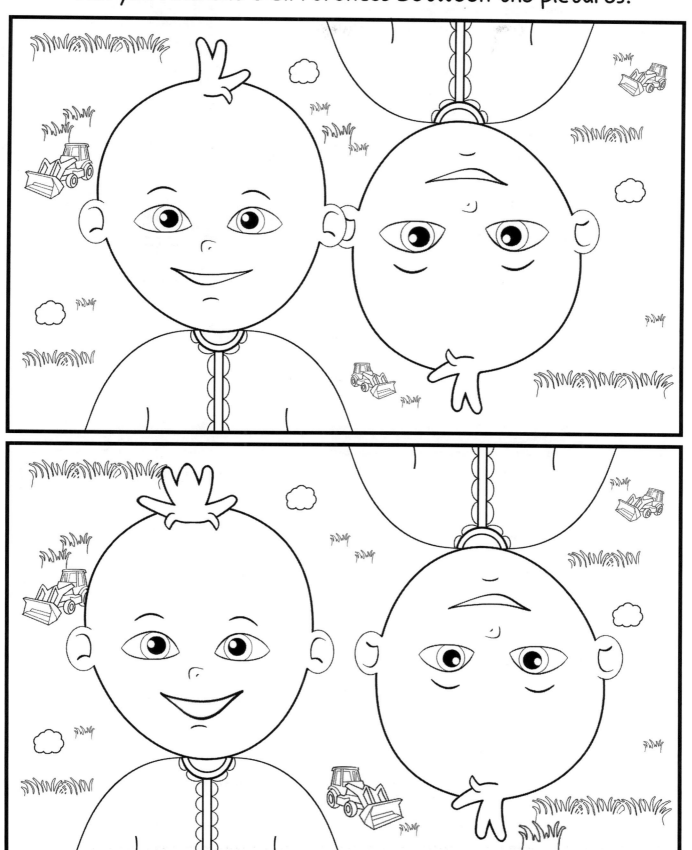

Draw a picture of your whole FAMILY.

Tips for Parents

Have the new babies bring the big brother a gift. This can be something small (e.g. a lollipop), but will be memorable for the older sibling.

Include big brother in daily tasks to make them feel like a helper (e.g. picking out diaper or holding the bottle).

During feeding/bathing time for the twins provide big brother with coloring/activity book to entertain and relax the older sibling.

The big brother may have some feelings of jealousy towards the twins. Try to provide the big brother with one-on-one time with a parent.

Provide positive reinforcement and praise to the big brother.

Ask for help from family, friends, & neighbors!

Made in the USA
Monee, IL
21 December 2023

50323225R00024